— THE —
FARTING ANIMALS
COLORING BOOK

Farts are funny!
Farting animals are even funnier...

Copyright © 2016 by Lake George Press
www.forgottenfairies.com

ISBN-13:978-1539486121
ISBN-10:1539486125

Other books by M.T. Lott

24695028R00026

Made in the USA
Lexington, KY
18 December 2018